CIRCLE
OF CARE

GW00715498

VERITAS
2000

First published 2000 by
Veritas Publications
7/8 Lower Abbey Street
Dublin 1

Copyright © Dublin World Day of the Sick Committee

ISBN 1 85390 359 0

British Library Cataloguing
in Publication Data.
A catalogue record for
this book is available
from the British Library.

With Special Thanks to:
Bishop Eamonn Walsh
Trish Conway
Martin Browne

Design: Bill Bolger
Printed in the Republic of Ireland by Betaprint Ltd, Dublin

Contents

Statue of Christ the King by the Artisanats des Monastéres de Bethléem

Foreword

Each year the Church celebrates World Day of the Sick. She is our Mother. And where will you find a mother if not with the child who is ill? And will she not show recognition to all who share her special concern to bring hope and relief to suffering?

From our first breath to our last we all pass through moments of need for loving care. Through our baptism we pledge to care for one another as Christ's hands and eyes and ears and voice. This pledge commits us to provide the best we can in our care for the sick. Jesus himself has shown us the way, and his example is depicted in Christian art as in the Icon opposite. The depth of his love is a full measure, pressed down and overflowing (Lk 6:8). It knows no half measures; it is ready to walk two miles when asked to go one (Mt 5:41). This is the love of Jesus who emptied himself to the point of death (Phil 2:7-8) in order to show how he loves us.

The heart of Christ draws us with him into a free and generous response to the call of his Father's love, even when that call beckons us through a valley of darkness into the light where all will be made new (Ps. 22:4). In that heart there is strength and dignity and peace. May it inspire us in our moments of suffering and in our care for one another.

✠ Desmond Connell
Archbishop of Dublin

Introduction

Within our community, there are few who are not touched in some way by the experiences of sickness or trauma. We only have to reflect for a moment to realise how immediate are those experiences, even within our own families. Ill-health is no respecter of persons, from the young to the elderly, tragedy strikes at random, impairing or taking away physical or mental ability. There are no concerns that are not the concerns of each of us when it comes to issues of health and well-being. Loss, whether through the death of a loved one or the realisation of human fragility, strikes to the core, throwing us into a lonely cycle of uncertainty and grief.

Those of us who grapple with the reality of suffering and impairment frequently feel isolated and separated from others. This is true, also, of those who are our carers. More than ever, there is a need for the experience of confirmation and community which supports us in coping with the stresses and distresses of disability and of bereavement, enabling us to meet the new challenges to live in faith, hope and love.

Those of us who minister to people who suffer in body or in mind, or to those who care for them, need to be open to their experiences and to their questions. We need to be open, also, to learn from their strengths and their wisdoms wrought in pain.

This book is a thoughtful and sensitive collection of services, or liturgies, for use in pastoral care. Its scope reaches out to include those who may feel most overlooked or forgotten in modern society and those who love them. Each of the services creates an opportunity for members of the community to meet together and to be mutually supportive, perhaps for the first time, in the wider context of God's healing intention.

The texts offered here – the scriptures, the hymns, the poems – give voice to the feelings that accompany a painful disruption of life's certainties. They describe the loss and the subsequent search for meaning attendant on such disruptions. They assure that, in God's world, nothing is pointless.

Included in the book is the message for the World Day of the Sick for the year 2000 from Pope John Paul II. In this message the Pope speaks of Jesus as one who was, in his own life, 'the good Samaritan'. In the story, as in his life, Jesus exemplifies what it means to be a neighbour and a companion. He is our model.

When we minister to the sick, or are ministered to, we stand together. And when we stand together, the Saviour stands with us. He has said so. This is what we believe and what brings us together. *Circle of Care* offers us an opportunity and the means to lighten the darkness with the healing light of Christ Jesus in this millennium year and the years to come.

Fr Maurice Reidy

Call Me By Name

A Naming Ceremony

INTRODUCTION

Baptism and the giving of a name 'are the rituals by which new members are welcomed into the Christian Community. This ceremony is an opportunity to name and honour children who died before or around the time of birth and who were never formally named or welcomed into the Christian community in baptism.

In the past, mistakes have been made and great hurt caused because of a lack of knowledge and understanding. We now understand much more about the processes of life as it begins in the womb – we can chart the development of this life right from the moment of conception to birth – and yet this knowledge increases rather than diminishes our wonder at the complexity and ultimate mystery of our existence as human beings.

Children who do not survive beyond the womb have participated in this great mystery, this great gift of life. For no matter how much scientific and medical expertise we have about the mechanics of life, the Spirit which gives us our being is still beyond our human understanding. The words spoken to Jeremiah in the

Old Testament are spoken to all of us: *'Before I formed you in the womb I knew you'.*

Those who, for whatever reason, do not survive beyond the first stage of life in a mother's womb are already fully known and enfolded in the personal love of God, in the palm of whose hand we are all held. These children are simply gone home before the rest of us.

Parents may well ask, in their initial anguish at the loss of their expected child, 'Why has this happened to us?'. Parents need to be comforted, to be assured that it is right and normal to mourn the child they conceived. The help and support of a caring community can be a source of strength to the family.

This ceremony might take place yearly, perhaps on the Feast of the Guardian Angels (2 October) or in early springtime. The occasion should be advertised widely, in local newspapers and on local radio stations, in addition to the parish bulletin.

The church should be decorated in bright colours, reflecting life and innocence. A central candle, decorated with fresh flowers, and placed on a welcome table, should be lighting as the families and their friends arrive.

SONG A familiar setting of the Gloria

GREETING

May Christ Jesus, who welcomed children and laid his hands in blessing upon them, fill you with his peace and be always with you. *And also with you.*

OPENING PRAYER

God, you formed man and woman in your own image and likeness and invited them to share with you in the creation of new life.

Let those who feel overwhelmed by the loss of that gift of new life find comfort in believing that you are with them in their moments of sorrow. We ask that they experience your healing presence and find solace through participating in this time of prayer. We ask this through the Good Shepherd, Jesus the Lord. *Amen.*

READING Matthew 25:34
Come, you who my Father has blessed, take as your heritage the kingdom prepared for you since the foundation of the world.

SONG Yahweh, I Know You Are Near (St Louis Jesuits)

The presider invites the parents of each child who is to be named to come forward.

God our loving Father is a faithful God who created us all after his own image. All things are of his making, all creation awaits the day of salvation. He has called each of us by name from all eternity.

The presider addresses each family in turn.

What name do you give your child?

The parents name their child. The presider gives a lighted candle to them and continues:

N., may the Lord bless you and keep you,
May he let his face shine on you and be gracious to you,
May he uncover his face to you and bring you peace.

The families return to their places and all stand and pray

LITANY
You became a little child for our sake, sharing our human life.
To you we pray:
Bless us and keep us, O Lord.

You welcomed children, promising them your kingdom.
To you we pray:
Bless us and keep us, O Lord.

You took upon yourself the suffering and death of us all.
To you we pray:
Bless us and keep us, O Lord.

THE LORD'S PRAYER
Together let us pray for strength for acceptance, and for the coming of the Kingdom in the words our Saviour taught us: *Our Father...*

FINAL PRAYER
God of kindness and compassion,
You created these children in your own image and likeness,
Bestowing on them the gift of life,
A gift that is transformed, but never taken away.
We entrust them to your everlasting love.

We pray for their parents.
You were with them in the time of happiness when they conceived their child.
Be with them now
and one day unite all parents and their children
in the peace and joy of your Kingdom.

We ask this through Christ, our Lord. *Amen.*

SONG   Holy Mary, Full Of Grace   (Jean-Paul Lécot)

Each family should receive a certificate, commemorating the naming of their child.

On the Palms of My Hands

Remembering Babies Who Died
Before or Around the Time of Birth

INTRODUCTION

As part of its centenary celebrations in 1994, the National
Maternity Hospital in Dublin's Holles Street organised a
Service of Remembrance for babies who died before or around the
time of birth. This took place in Saint Andrew's Church, Westland
Row, during the month of November. Large numbers of people,
from various parts of the country, attended the service. This affirmed
the conviction of those who work closely with parents that an
opportunity to remember and to grieve would be appreciated.

An Oak Tree blessed at the first celebration was planted in Archbishop Ryan Park, Merrion Square, and a bed of snowdrops was planted around it. A commemorative stone inscribed with a poem, *Tree Of Life*, specially written by Eavan Boland for the service, was placed there as a permanent memorial to the babies. It is a place of calm where people can come to be quiet, to remember and to reflect.

It would be fitting to invite hospital staff – in their uniforms, where appropriate – to be the ministers of hospitality for this service. They should greet people on arrival and invite them to write the names of those to be remembered on a sheet of paper. These names will be presented during the service. They also offer a service sheet and a small candle to all present.

SONG Christ Be Beside Me (James Quinn / Gaelic)

GREETING
From the God of all consolation, light and peace
be with you all.
And also with you.

WELCOME
A representative from a maternity hospital, or another caring agency, welcomes the people and introduces the service.

OPENING PRAYER
Let us pray,

Tender and loving God,
be with those who gather in sadness today to remember.
We thank you for the gift of life, however brief,
and we place our children safely in your care.
We make our prayer through Christ, Our Lord. *Amen.*

The following readings and prayers are spoken by parents, grandparents and siblings of babies who have died.

READING Isaiah 49:14-16

Can a woman forget her baby at the breast,
Feel no pity for the child she has borne?
Even if these were to forget,
I shall not forget you.
Look, I have engraved you on the palms of my hands.

SONG I Will Never Forget You (Carey Landry)
During the song half the people are invited to come forward and place their lighted candles in the sanctuary, creating the image of a crib, into which the names will be placed later.

PRAYER

Loving God,
We believe that these children are with you.
We trust in your promise to keep all of us in mind.
In these moments of remembrance, it is love that makes us cry and it is your healing hand which wipes our tears away.
Keep us strong in your love.
We make our prayer through Christ, Our Lord. *Amen.*

READING Romans 8:38-39

For I am certain of this: neither death nor life, nor angels, nor principalities, nothing already in existence and nothing still to come, nor any power, nor the heights nor the depths, nor any created thing whatever, will be able to come between us and the love of God, known to us in Christ Jesus our Lord.

SONG Abide With Me (Lyte / Monk)

At this time the remainder of the people are encouraged to come forward with their candles.

GOSPEL John 14:5-7

Thomas said, 'Lord, we do not know where you are going, so how can we know the way?' Jesus said: 'I am the Way, I am Truth and Life. No one can come to the Father except through me. If you know me, you will know my Father too. From this moment you know him and have seen him.'

LITANY *Liodán an Rísigh* Seán Ó Cearbhaill
RESPONSE Déan trócaire is trua

In the tears of the broken
When no word is spoken
O God of all tokens
Déan trócaire is trua.   r/

In the night of my sorrow
Some hope I will borrow
From the God of tomorrow
Déan trócaire is trua.   r/

In the time of leaving
When an end comes to grieving
Dear Lord of Believing
Déan trócaire is trua.   r/

PRESENTATION OF NAMES

During the singing of the hymn, the names of babies being remembered are brought to the altar by parents and hospital staff.

SONG Shepherd Song (Chrysogonous Waddell)
      REFRAIN Jesus Good Shepherd, Call Us By Name.

POEM Tree of Life
Instrumental music accompanies the recitation of one of the poems specially composed for the National Maternity Hospital services.

A tree on a moonless night
has no sap or colour.

It has no flower and no fruit.
It waits for the sun to find them.
I cannot find you
in this dark hour
dear child

wait
for dawn
to make us clear to one another.

Let the sun
inch above the rooftops.

Let love be the light that shows again
the blossom to the root.
       (Eavan Boland)

POEM Elegy for Deirdre Ann

To those realms where you abide
in brightness, Deirdre Ann, I send
this message on the stellar tide
so you might mend.
Though words of mine do not contain
the secret balm to soothe a soul,
of course, considering such pain,
and yet the bowl
of tears fills up next door with all
the sorrow of your parents left,
to find the needful where-with-all
to live bereft –

And I am driven by their love
that sings in all the winter trees
to this small room that lies above
and aim to please

The shattered heart of Hugh and Julie,
brave amid the cold debris
of your coming here unruly
not rising free,

And Deirdre Ann, though grief attends
your coming in and going out, my dear,
and no needle really mends,
you are loved here.

        (Sebastian Barry)

Comforting God,

We thank you for the precious time we have spent together in remembrance. Help us to face each day with trust in your healing and comforting presence. *Amen.*

Final Blessing

The Lord be with you.

And also with you.

May the God who never forgets keep you, and those you hold dear, in the palm of his hand. May you know his gentleness and compassion; and may the blessing of Almighty God, the Father, and the Son, ✠ and the Holy Spirit, come down upon you and remain with you always. *Amen.*

Song Lord of All Hopefulness (Struther/Gaelic)

Parents and family members might be invited to plant a flower bulb in remembrance after the service. A memorial garden could be developed, either near the hospital or near the church.

Learn Through Children's Eyes

Praying for and with Sick Children

INTRODUCTION

Sickness in children is a reality for many families. Lifelong and serious illness in a child is one of life's most difficult challenges, especially when it leads to uncertainty about the future, or a diminished physical quality of life or early death.

Nature conditions us to expect young life to be free of pain, disability or worry. Technical and medical expertise lead many to believe anything is possible, whereas the reality of lifelong illness forces us to live with smaller goals.

A sick child affects everyone in his or her circle. The atmosphere at home, in the family, among friends and neighbours, or at school is often different, because sickness in a child raises questions about life and its meaning. We can question God, our beliefs and our values. Priorities and perspectives can change. What once seemed urgent and important suddenly takes second place to the immediate needs of the sick child.

When you take a child by the hand you might feel that you are the protector, but it may be that you are also the one who is receiving, because when you look into the eyes of a child living with illness you often see not just their beauty, but also a glimpse of what really matters in life – trust, security, love, faith and hope.

The setting for this service should be bright and cheerful. Colourful balloons, streamers, or artwork by children could adorn the space.

THE LITURGY IS DIVIDED INTO THREE SECTIONS:

I   Someone To Watch Over Me

II   Your Will Be Done, Not Mine

III Scorn Not His Simplicity

SONG As I Kneel Before You   (Maria Parkinson)

OPENING PRAYER
Father of tenderness and compassion,
you sent your Son to share our human nature,
to redeem all people, and to heal the sick.

Look with love on your children who are sick.
Support them with your power,
give them hope in times of suffering
and keep them always in your care.

We ask this through Christ, our Lord. *Amen.*

I – 'Someone to watch over me'

SONG I Have a Dream (ABBA)

REFLECTION
A young person could be invited to tell his or her story of living with illness and the place of faith in that experience.

SONG On Eagle's Wings (Frank Andersen)

PRAYER *To My Guardian Angel*
You helped me when I needed help
You protected me when I fell
You listened to me when I was down
We laughed when I was up
You were there when I needed you
Especially at night
You gave me strength when I needed it
Even though I can't give you anything, you don't mind
You were watching over me when I was having tests
Thank you for watching over me.

(Janice, age 13)

INSTRUMENTAL Someone to Watch Over Me (George Gershwin)

II – 'Your Will Be Done, Not Mine'

READING Luke 22:39-44
He then left to make his way as usual to the Mount of Olives, with the disciples following. When he reached the place he said to them, 'Pray not to be put to the test'.

Then he withdrew from them, about a stone's throw away, and knelt down and prayed. 'Father,' he said, 'if you are willing, take this cup away from me. Nevertheless, let your will be done, not mine.' Then an angel appeared to him coming from heaven to give him strength. In his anguish he prayed even more earnestly, and his sweat fell to the ground like great drops of blood.

REFLECTION
A parent could be invited to share his or her experiences of coping with the illness of a child and its effect on his or her faith.

SONG Tears in Heaven (Eric Clapton)

PARENT'S PRAYER
Lord, I am very angry today as I try to cope with my child's illness. You prayed in your agony Lord to let this chalice pass. Give me the strength to say with you 'let your will be done, not mine'.

SONG Pity Then the Child (Liam Lawton)

III – 'Scorn Not His Simplicity'

READING 2 Cor 4:7-10
But we hold this treasure in pots of earthenware, so that the immensity of the power is God's and not our own. We are subjected to every kind of hardship, but never distressed; we see no way out but we never despair; we are pursued but never cut off; knocked down, but still have some life in us; always we carry with us in our body the death of Jesus so that the life of Jesus, too, may be visible in our body.

REFLECTION

A care worker is invited to speak about sickness and children and to offer some insights based on those experiences.

SONG   Scorn Not His Simplicity   (Phil Coulter)

PRAYER

God bless all the nurses
Who try to make us well
They always come running
When we ring the bell.

God bless all the doctors
And the television in our room
God bless all the cleaning ladies
Who come round with their broom.
     (Adrian, age 12)

CONCLUDING PRAYER

Lord, give all sick children the inner strength to cope with the pressures that their illness brings. Help them to accept the love and care which their families have for them during this difficult time and give them the courage to let their parents know they love them. We ask this through Christ, our Lord. Amen.

SONG   Suffer Little Children   (Philip Green)

Come Back to Life

A Service of Prayer to Highlight Drug Awareness

The Return of the Prodigal by Rembrandt

Introduction

European Drug Prevention Week 1998 was marked in a variety of ways by interested groups throughout the country. The Church wished to afford an opportunity for people to come together in a context of prayer to listen, to reflect and to pray about this issue. Parishes were invited to design their own prayer service to be celebrated during the week using the model presented here. The background for the liturgy that follows emerged from a meeting with a representative group with experience of drugs programmes, addicts and those who suffer collateral damage as a result of the misuse of drugs.

Who will be there?

It is vital to involve a group of interested people in the preparation of this liturgy. This core group might come from a local school whose involvement might be informed by their awareness of drugs. It would be useful, where possible, to include relatives of addicts and, given the appropriate circumstances, addicts themselves at another stage of the process. The invitation to attend would come from this core group, who would also help with the publicity. Use of local radio stations is recommended where young people could speak to each other on the issue and extend the invitation. It is not, however, a liturgy exclusively for young people, as this is a community issue, but their input would be a crucial component.

Where will it be?

The number expected to attend would determine the space to be used for such a service. A small oratory, a meeting room or local hall might be more suitable than a large church with a small number present. The venue must be decorated and adapted to make the atmosphere warm, friendly and prayerful.

Materials

Use of images, symbols and colour adds to the celebration. Light and darkness can be used very effectively. Use of a hollow cross is suggested, into which lighted candles are placed by those present during the ceremony.

The story of the return of the prodigal son from Saint Luke's Gospel is central to the liturgy, as it will be paralleled at each step by real experiences and stories. Therefore, a good central focal point would be a large print of Rembrandt's *The Return of the Prodigal,* available from Veritas or Cathedral Books. Veritas also have a small prayer card, with the Rembrandt image on one side and the Serenity Prayer on the other, which can be used in the celebration.

WELCOME

The welcome is an essential element in the celebration and should be discreet and warm. A programme for the service will ensure participation and help those who feel unfamiliar in the environment and structure of the liturgy. All present receive a candle on arrival. Those who wish to light an additional candle to remember people who died as a result of drugs can be invited to do so at a portable shrine near the door, as they are coming in. This is later brought into the centre of the prayer space.

I – Prodigal Story

SONG Be Not Afraid (Bob Dufford)

STORY based on Luke 15:11
The opening part of the parable of the Prodigal is told in story form. The 'storyteller' should embellish the Gospel text, highlighting it as the story of one who, though much loved, wanted more and thought that freedom and money would win him happiness.

Sample
Jesus loved to tell stories and he often used them to make a point. One of the most famous of these is the story of a man who had two sons. He loved both of them dearly, and it is clear that they enjoyed a

good life, with plenty of food, servants and employment. The younger one became restless and asked his father for his portion of the inheritance. After a few days, he gathered all his possessions together and set off for another country, far away, where he squandered everything.

This can then be followed by the parallel story of a parent describing their child before their involvement with drugs.

During a period of reflection, a piece of instrumental music is played.

PRAYER
Tender God,
Give us the insight to appreciate what we have received.
Give us the humility to accept that we are loved.
Give us the courage to face up to our difficulties and insecurities.
Walk with us, now and always. *Amen.*

II – Prodigal Story

SONG My Son Has Gone Away (Bob Dufford)
(or any traditional Irish 'Caoineadh').

STORY Luke 15:12-20
When he had spent all of his money, that country experienced a severe famine, and now he began to feel the pinch; so he hired himself out to one of the local inhabitants who put him on his farm to feed the pigs. And he would willingly have filled himself with the husks the pigs were eating but no one would let him have them. Then he came to his senses and said, 'How many of my father's hired men have all the food they want and more, and here am I dying of hunger! I will leave this place and go to my father and say:

Father, I have sinned against heaven and against you; I no longer deserve to be called your son; treat me as one of your hired men.' So he left the place and went back to his father.

This is followed by the parallel story of the experience of an addict, if possible, or one who can describe the pain and disillusionment which drugs cause.

During a period of reflection, a piece of instrumental music is played.

INTERCESSIONS
Members of the assembly could be invited to offer intercessions for loved ones affected by drugs.

SONG O Lord Hear My Prayer (Taizé)

REMEMBRANCE
The shrine for those who died is then placed in the centre of the space.

SONG Jesus Remember Me (Taizé)

III – Prodigal Story

SONG The God Of Life (Liam Lawton)

STORY Luke 15:20-24
While he was still a long way off, his father saw him and was moved with pity. He ran to the boy, clasped him in his arms and kissed him. Then his son said, 'Father, I have sinned against heaven and against you. I no longer deserve to be called your son.' But the father said to his servants, 'Quick! Bring out the best robe and put it on him; put a ring on his finger and sandals on his feet. Bring the calf we have been

fattening, and kill it; we will celebrate by having a feast, because this son of mine was dead and has come back to life; he was lost and is found.' And they began to celebrate.

This is then followed by the parallel story of the experience of help offered and accepted without condition. This could involve a counsellor or a friend who was faithful through the experience.

SONG Servant Song (Richard Gillard)

PRAYER *All*
God grant me the serenity
To accept the things I cannot change,
Courage to change the things I can,
And the wisdom to know the difference.

SONG Healer of My Soul (John Michael Talbot)
       or
       All Will Be Well (Steven C. Warner)

CANDLE CEREMONY
Those present are invited to light their candles and place them in the hollow cross. The mixture of light and darkness is an expression of the reality of the ongoing story, which does not always have a happy ending or the one we expect.

SONG Your Love Is Never Ending (Marty Haugen)

CONCLUSION
All leave in their own time and receive the small Prodigal prayer card at the door. Refreshments might be laid on to allow people to chat and seek further information or help. Those present who are

vulnerable need to be looked after, as the experience could be very moving for them. It is important to attempt to close wounds that have been opened and allow people the grace to continue their journey.

Bishop Brendan Comiskey, in a reflection on this Gospel story, draws attention to the gift of the sandals which the father gave his son:

'Sandals are God's guarantee that there are no strings attached to our welcome home. With sandals, we are forever free to leave again!'

The best we can hope for is to be able to help another stand on their own two feet again or to prevent others from throwing their freedom away.

SUGGESTED REFLECTIONS

Lord If Only You Could Listen
Lord, if only you could listen and hear confusion in my mind,
Would you break down and cry for me,
Would you break down and die for me?
And Lord, if you could know the feeling when life begins to get me down,
Would you break down and cry for me,
Would you break down and die for me?

And Lord, to live from day to day,
Would never help me find my way,
O Lord will you take my hand and lead me there,
To your side forever, 'ever my Lord?

Our Deepest Fear

Our deepest fear is not that we are inadequate. Our deepest fear is that we are powerful beyond measure. It is our light, not our darkness, that most frightens. We ask ourselves, who am I to be brilliant, gorgeous, talented and fabulous? Actually, who are you not to be?

You are a child of God – your playing small doesn't serve the world. There is nothing enlightened about shrinking so that other people will not feel insecure around you. We were born to make manifest the glory of God that is within us. It is not in just some of us: It is in everyone and as we let our own light shine, we unconsciously give people permission to do the same.

As we are liberated from our own fear, our presence automatically liberates others.

(Nelson Mandela)

The Killer

You stick the needles in your vein,
You think it might relieve the pain,
Then later when it wears away,
You're like you were at the start of the day.

The cramps return and the sweating starts,
You feel the need deep in your heart,
You run to your nearest dealer and get some more,
Then when you get home it's time to score,
You put the needle in your arm,
Convincing yourself it will do you no harm,

But if you take a closer look,
You'll see that you are really hooked,
Nobody can save you if you don't care,
So you go to the mirror and have a good stare,
Your cheeks have started to sink into your face,
You're beginning to look as thin as a rake,
Your eyes are in the back of your head,
To be honest with you, you really look dead.

So, if you want help, do it now,
You don't know what to do - ask someone how,
Listen to what I have said,
Get out before you end up dead.
    (Laura Byrne)

Shattering The Silence

A Journey Together Towards Hope

INTRODUCTION

HIV is touching the lives of an increasing number within society. Many people, if they haven't been affected directly within their own family circle, know of other families whose son, daughter, husband, wife, mother, father, partner or friend is living with the virus, or has died. As we have learned more about the virus, our initial fears have given way gradually to understanding and our understanding to compassion, though very many people with the virus still feel isolated and alienated.

All whose lives are affected by HIV/AIDS are asked to allow us walk with them on their journey. It should be acknowledged that for many people living with HIV or AIDS the Church is not a welcome fellow traveller. It is perceived in many of its official statements on HIV/AIDS to have caused pain and hurt. While it would not be respected were it to abandon or compromise its teaching role, its tone has too often been insensitive, to the extent that compassion has been overshadowed or lost. As brothers and sisters equal in the eyes of God, we need to walk together in respect, so that we may all be enriched in our mutual giving and receiving.

'Be close to the sick and their families,
acting in such a way that those being
put to the test will never feel marginalised'
      (Pope John Paul II - World Day of the Sick 1996)

The following texts could be used during a Mass in which people living with HIV or AIDS are being remembered in a special way.

SONG Gather Us In (Marty Haugen)

Litany of Praise
Lord Jesus, you reach out to all in need of healing:
Lord, have mercy.
Lord, have mercy.

Lord Jesus, you offer the hand of reconciliation to all who stray:
Lord, have mercy.
Lord, have mercy.

Lord Jesus, you welcome the outcasts to your table:
Lord, have mercy.
Lord, have mercy.

OPENING PRAYER
All-powerful and ever-living God,
We find security in your forgiveness.
Give us serenity and peace of mind;
May we rejoice in your gifts of kindness
And use them always for your glory and our good.
We ask this in the name of Jesus, the Lord. *Amen.*

FIRST READING   Isaiah 58:7-18

Thus says the Lord: Share your bread with the hungry, and shelter the homeless poor, clothe the person you see to be naked and turn not from your own kin. Then will your light shine like the dawn and your wound be quickly healed over.

Your integrity will go before you and the glory of the Lord behind you. Cry, and the Lord will answer, call, and he will say, 'I am here'. If you do away with the yoke, the clenched fist, the wicked word, if you give your bread to the hungry and relief to the oppressed, your light will rise in the darkness, and your shadows become like noon.

RESPONSORIAL PSALM   On Eagle's Wings   (Michael Joncas)

SECOND READING   Titus 3:4-7

When the kindness and love of God our Saviour for humankind were revealed, it was not because he was concerned with any righteous action we might have done ourselves; it was for no reason except his own compassion that he saved us, by means of the cleansing water of rebirth and by renewing us with the Holy Spirit which he has so generously poured over us through Jesus Christ our Saviour. He did this so that we should be justified by his grace, to become heirs looking forward to inheriting eternal life.

GOSPEL   Luke 6:27

Jesus said to his disciples: 'I say this to you who are listening: Love your enemies, do good to those who hate you, bless those who curse you, pray for those who treat you badly. Be compassionate as your heavenly Father is compassionate. Do not judge and you will not be judged yourselves; do not condemn, and you will not be condemned yourselves; grant pardon, and you will be pardoned. Give, and there will be gifts for you. A full measure, pressed down, shaken together,

and running over, will be poured into your lap, because the amount
you measure out is the amount you will be given back'.

PRAYER OVER THE GIFTS
God our Father,
Your love guides every moment of our lives.
Accept the prayers and gifts we offer for our sick brothers
and sisters;
Restore them to health and turn our anxiety for them into joy.

*Option D of the Eucharistic Prayer for Various Needs and Occasions –
Jesus, The Compassion of God – might be used.*

COMMUNION SONG Healer of My Soul (John Michael Talbot)

PRAYER AFTER COMMUNION
God our Father, our help in human weakness,
Show our sick brothers and sisters the power of your loving care.
In your kindness make them well. We ask this… *Amen.*

REFLECTION *Blowing the Image*
There's a lot of dirty deals
going down
It's not just black and white
If you've got a voice
Then please use it right
There's a lot of silent people
out there
They're wounded and they're hurt
So let us shatter the silence.

I'm blowing the image
I'm coming clean
I've just come through
some crazy dream
I'm HIV-Positive as can be
So don't go ringing your bell
when you see me
So don't go ringing your bell
when you see me.

There's a lot of lonely kids
out there
The streets are cold and
they're bare
think tourniquet
and needles
Are the answer to their dreams
Before you take the plunge
my child
Pay heed to what I say
because I've been down
that road to hell
There must be a better way.
                    (Christy Salinger)

O Comfort My People

A Healing Service

This service was prepared to offer an opportunity for healing to all who suffer as a result of abuse of any kind – physical, sexual, psychological or emotional. The key elements are listening, reflecting and the ceremonies of light, blessing and planting. A Candle of Healing, decorated with fresh flowers in gentle colours is placed in a prominent position in the sanctuary.

This service was first celebrated in St Andrew's Church, Westland Row, Dublin, on 18 May 1998. Following the ceremony a Rose Bed was inaugurated in Archbishop Ryan Park, Merrion Square, to mark the occasion and to provide a place of hope and beauty where people can come to be quiet, to reflect or to pray.

ENTRANCE SONG   O Comfort My People   (Chrysogonous Waddell)

WELCOME

SONG Healer of My Soul (John Michael Talbot)

POEM Bubba Esther
She was still upset,
she wanted to tell me,
she kept remembering
the terrible hands:

how she came, a young girl
of seventeen, a freckled
fair-skinned Jew from Kovno
to Hamburg with her uncle
and stayed in an old house
and waited while he bought
the steamship tickets
so they could sail to America.

and how he came into her room
sat down on the bed, touched
her waist, took her by the
breast, said for a kiss
she could have her ticket,
her skirts were rumpled, her
petticoat torn, his teeth were
broken, his breath full of
onions, she was ashamed
still ashamed, lying
eighty years later
in the hospital bed,
trying to tell me,
trembling, weeping with anger.
          (Ruth Whitman)

Psalm 31

Response   The Lord is my light and my help

In you, O Lord I take refuge,
Let me never be put to shame.
In your justice, set me free,
Hear me and rescue me.   r/

Be a rock of refuge for me,
A mighty stronghold to save me,
For you are my rock, my stronghold.
For your name's sake, lead me and guide me. r/

Have mercy on me, O Lord,
For I am in distress
Tears wasted my eyes,
My throat and my heart.   r/

For my life spent with sorrow
And my years with sighs.
Affliction has broken down my strength
And my bones waste away.   r/

How great is the goodness, Lord,
That you keep for those who fear you,
That you show to those who trust you
In the sight of men.   r/

Be strong, let your heart take courage,
All who hope in the Lord.   r/

READING Romans 8:31-35; 37-39

If God is for us, who can be against us? Since he did not spare his own son, but gave him for the sake of all of us, then can we not expect that with him he will freely give us all his gifts? Who can bring any accusation against those that God has chosen? When God grants saving justice who can condemn? Are we not sure that it is Christ Jesus, who died – yes and more, who was raised from the dead and is at God's right hand – and who is adding his plea for us? Can anything cut us off from the love of Christ – can hardships or distress, or persecution, or lack of food and clothing, or threats or violence.

We come through all these things triumphantly victorious, by the power of him who loved us. For I am certain of this: neither death nor life, nor angels, nor principalities, nothing already in existence and nothing still to come, nor any power, nor the heights nor the depths, nor any created thing whatever, will be able to come between us and the love of God, known to us in Christ Jesus our Lord.

CANDLE SERVICE

All are invited to come forward and light their night-light from the Candle of Healing. The following are sung during this part of the ceremony.

SONG Servant Song (Richard Gillard)

SONG Pity Then the Child (Liam Lawton)

GOSPEL Mark 10:13-16

People were bringing little children to Jesus, for him to touch them. The disciples scolded them, but when Jesus saw this he was indignant and said to them, 'Let the little children come to me; do not stop them; for it is to such as these that the kingdom of God belongs. In truth, I tell you, anyone who does not welcome the kingdom of God like a little child will never enter it.' Then he embraced them, laid his hands on them and gave them his blessing.

SONG   On Eagle's Wings   (Michael Joncas)

ADDRESS
This would bring together the strands of the different readings and reflections. It could be given by someone with experience in pastoral care and healing.

INTERCESSIONS
Gathered in faith as the Body of Christ we confidently present our prayers of healing to God, our Creator:

'If you want to you can heal me' – We pray for all those who have been abused physically, mentally, emotionally or sexually:
>   That God will heal and comfort them.
>   Let us pray to the Lord:
>   *Lord, hear our prayer.*

'If you want to you can heal me' – We pray for all in the healing professions who minister to those who suffer as a result of violence or abuse:
>   That God will give them an abundance of love, compassion and wisdom.
>   Let us pray to the Lord:
>   *Lord, hear our prayer.*

'If you want to you can heal me' - We pray for the Spirit of wisdom:
> That it will enlighten the minds of all people and lead to a
> growth in awareness and a determination to put an end to all
> acts of violence and abuse
> Let us pray to the Lord:
> *Lord, hear our prayer.*

'If you want to you can heal me' – We pray for those for whom the
burden of violence and abuse has proved too much to bear:
> That the God of love and mercy grant them everlasting
> peace and happiness.
> Let us pray to the Lord:
> *Lord, hear our prayer.*

> Gentle and ever-loving God,
> Listen to the prayers of your people who offer them in the
> Spirit, through Christ Our Lord. *Amen.*

A PRAYER FOR INNER PEACE AND TRANSFORMATION Joyce **Rupp**

SONG An tAiséirí (Traditional)

BLESSING
*Those present are invited to come forward and holy water is used to mark
them with the Sign of the Cross, as a gesture of healing. During this rite
the following is sung:*

SONG Lay Your Hands (Carey Landry)

CLOSING PRAYER
God our rock and our strength,
Your gift of courage enabled us to be here today.

The atmosphere of trust allowed the unspeakable to be said.
Help us to live with our painful memories.
May we support each other as we move from this place.
We pray in the name of Jesus, your compassion made flesh,
Who lives with you and the Spirit, now and for ever. Amen.

SONG The Clouds' Veil (Liam Lawton)

HELPLINES:

AMEN   Confidential Advice line for Men in Violent Relationships
Telephone (046) 23718

CARI   Children At Risk in Ireland
Telephone (01) 830 8529

CHANCELLERY   Archbishop's House, Dublin 9
Telephone (01) 837 3732 or 8379 253

CHILDLINE   c/o ISPCC
Freephone 1800 25 00 25

CURA Nationwide Freephone 1850 622 262

FAOISEAMH Helpline Freephone 1800 33 12 34

LIFE LoCall 1850 281 281

RAPE CRISIS CENTRE   Freephone 1800 77 88 88

VICTIM SUPPORT Freephone 1800 61 66 17

WOMEN'S SUPPORT Telephone (01) 286 6163

From Darkness To Dawn

Resources for a Liturgy on Mental Illness

INTRODUCTION

Mental health problems can affect anyone. Unlike arthritis or asthma it may not be obvious that a person suffers from them. However, this can be a disadvantage because sometimes society and the people around the person do not always recognise and understand the disability.

As in the case of most illnesses and disabilities, any possible cure requires the co-operation and help of a team. Team members are parents, family members, employers and employees, neighbours and friends. The other members of the team are the health professionals. They are the ones who will provide counselling, the most up-to-date drugs and a recovery or aftercare programme.

Many people with mental illnesses find great support in their Christian faith. Even when they cannot pray for themselves they often appreciate the intercession of others. It is not always easy to find a meaning to the suffering that touches our lives. The power of the Word of God and the nourishment of the Eucharist offer healing and strength in the face of anguish.

ENTRANCE SONG The Lord is My Light (Taizé)

OPENING PRAYER
God our Father,
Look upon us with love.
You redeem us and make us your children in Christ.
Give us true freedom and bring us to the inheritance you promised.
We ask this... *Amen.*

FIRST READING Job 3:20-26
Why give light to a man of grief?
Why give life to those bitter of heart,
why long for a death that never comes,
and hunt for it more than for a buried treasure?
They would be glad to see the grave-mound
and shout with joy if they reached the tomb.

Why give light to one who does not see his way,
whom God shuts in all alone?

My only food is sighs,

and my groans pour out like water.

Whatever I fear comes true,

whatever I dread befalls me.

For me, there is no calm, no peace;

my torments banish rest.

SONG On Eagle's Wings (Michael Joncas)

SECOND READING James 5:13-18

Any one of you who is in trouble should pray; anyone in good spirits should sing a psalm. Any one of you is ill should send for the elders of the church, and they must anoint the sick person with oil in the name of the Lord and pray over him. The prayer of faith will save the sick person and the Lord will raise him up again; and if he has committed any sins, he will be forgiven. So confess your sins to one another, and pray for one another to be cured; the heartfelt prayer of someone upright works very powerfully. Elijah was a human being as frail as ourselves – he prayed earnestly for it not to rain, and no rain fell for three and a half years; then he prayed again and the sky gave rain and the earth gave crops.

GOSPEL John 11:32-44

Mary went to Jesus, and as soon as she saw him she threw herself at his feet, saying, 'Lord, if you had been here, my brother would not have died.' At the sight of her tears, and those of the Jews who had come with her, Jesus was greatly distressed, and with a profound sigh he said, 'Where have you put him?' They said, 'Lord, come and see.' Jesus wept; and the Jews said, 'See how much he loved him!' But there were some who remarked, 'He opened the eyes of the blind man. Could he not have prevented this man's death?' Sighing again, Jesus reached the tomb: It was a cave with a stone to close the opening. Jesus said, 'Take the stone away.' Martha, the dead man's sister, said to him, 'Lord, by now he will smell; this is the fourth day since he died.' Jesus replied, 'Have I not told you that if you believe you will see the glory of God?' So they took the stone away. Then Jesus lifted up his eyes and said: 'Father I thank you for hearing my prayer. I myself knew that you hear me always, but I speak for the sake of all these who are standing around me, so that they may believe it was you who sent me.'

When he had said this, he cried in a loud voice, 'Lazarus, come out!' The dead man came out, his feet and hands bound with strips of material and a cloth over his face. Jesus said to them, 'Unbind him, let him go free.'

PRAYER OVER THE GIFTS
Lord,
Accept these gifts from your family.
May we hold fast to the life you have given us
And come to the eternal gifts your promise.
We ask this... *Amen.*

Option B of the Eucharistic Prayer for Various Needs and Occasions – God guides the Church on the way to salvation – might be used.

PRAYER AFTER COMMUNION
Lord,
You give us the body and blood of your Son to renew your life within us.
In your mercy, assure our redemption and bring us to the eternal life we celebrate in this Eucharist. We ask this... *Amen.*

USEFUL CONTACT GROUPS

Detailed information on Mental Health can be found in the Directory of Mental Health Services which is available in Public Libraries and Eastern Health Board offices.

AWARE

147 Phibsborough Road, Dublin 7

Helpline (01) 6791711 (Mon-Fri 10am-10pm)

THE ALZHEIMERS SOCIETY OF IRELAND

Telephone (01) 288 1282

DA – DEPRESSED ANONYMOUS

Dublin Central Mission, Lower Abbey Street, Dublin 1

GROW

167 Capel Street, Dublin 1

Telephone (01) 8734029

HUNTINGTON'S DISEASE ASSOCIATION OF IRELAND

Freephone 1800 39 39 39

MENTAL HEALTH ASSOCIATION OF IRELAND

Telephone (01) 284 1166

RECOVERY

Telephone (01) 455 9074

SCHIZOPHRENIA ASSOCIATION OF IRELAND

Telephone (01) 676 1988

Hope In The Face Of Suicide

A Service of Remembrance, Consolation and Hope

INTRODUCTION

The Light of Hope shines deeply in each human heart, even in the darkest moments. Sometimes, however, that light is hidden and life seems to lose all purpose. Suicide can, in such circumstances, seem to offer the only escape from intense human suffering.

Suicide is a great human tragedy and a devastating reality for many families. As many as 433 deaths were recorded as suicide in Ireland in 1997. The vast majority of these were men. Ireland has the fastest growing rate of youth suicide in the world. Almost one in four people who commit suicide are between fifteen and twenty-four years old.

No words can capture the intense grief of those bereaved by suicide. At first the deliberate nature of the act is difficult to accept or understand. There may be feelings of anger, guilt, anxiety and the sense of irreplaceable loss. Then there is the prolonged and painful search for some explanation. Sometimes it is only with the benefit of hindsight that some understanding is achieved. In time, with support and God's help, inner strength is discovered, helping those left behind to survive the tragedy.

It is a reality that many people actively contemplate suicide. They experience a deep sense of hopelessness and despair. While suicide may seem the only route to take, consider instead that you have reached a crossroads or a turning point. You don't have to feel that you are facing this frightening situation alone. Know that there are people who care about you, there are people you can talk to. There is always help available, help that can rekindle the light of hope, the sense of inner warmth that makes life possible.

This service is made up of three sections: Remembering those who have taken their own lives, comforting those bereaved through suicide and offering hope. Candles are given to all as they arrive.

I – Remembrance

The Paschal Candle is lighting in the sanctuary, surrounded by greenery and signs of new life. A bowl of incense burns nearby. Quiet instrumental music is played

WELCOME
The presider welcomes those gathered and introduces the service.

SONG Jesus Remember Me (Taizé)

LETTER OF REMEMBRANCE

My dear _____,

As you read this letter, we would like you to know that we miss you and that so much has changed because of you. We always thought this sort of thing happened to other people, not us.

Maybe, in your heart, you thought you were doing us a favour by taking your life. What hurt most is that you never really said 'Goodbye' or gave us a chance to say 'Goodbye'. We have cried as we tried to understand your despair, your misery.

At times we have been angry with you for what you did to yourself, for what you did to us. At times we felt responsible for your death. We have searched for what we did or failed to do, for the clues we missed.

Yet we know that we didn't make your choice. We are learning to stop feeling responsible for your death. If we were responsible for you, you'd still be alive.

We all think of you so often, even when it hurts to remember. We are really lonely for your presence and whenever we hear your songs, we still cry for you. We feel sad that you're not here to share so many moments with us. That's when our mornings have no beginning and our nights seem long as winter.

Slowly though, it's getting less hard. We try to remember the good times. Maybe you've seen us smile a little more. We're learning to live again, realising that we cannot die because you chose to die. We pray that you are at peace. At the end of our days we look forward to being with you again — Peace.

PRAYER

Lord our God, you are always faithful and quick to show mercy.
We pray for our brothers and sisters who were suddenly and violently taken from us. Come swiftly to their aid, have mercy on

them and comfort their families and friends by the power and protection of the cross. We ask this through Christ our Lord. Amen.

SONG There Is A Place   (Liam Lawton)

READING Romans 8:31-35, 37-39

If God is for us, who can be against us? Since he did not spare his own son, but gave him for the sake of all of us, then can we not expect that with him he will freely give us all his gifts? Who can bring any accusation against those that God has chosen? When God grants saving justice who can condemn? Are we not sure that it is Christ Jesus, who died — yes and more, who was raised from the dead and is at God's right hand — and who is adding his plea for us? Can anything cut us off from the love of Christ — can hardships or distress, or persecution, or lack of food and clothing, or threats or violence.

We come through all these things triumphantly victorious, by the power of him who loved us. For I am certain of this: neither death nor life, nor angels, nor principalities, nothing already in existence and nothing still to come, nor any power, nor the heights nor the depths, nor any created thing whatever, will be able to come between us and the love of God, known to us in Christ Jesus our Lord.

CANDLE CEREMONY
All light candles received as part of the welcome and place them on a Taizé cross placed on the ground.

SONG I Know That My Redeemer Liveth   (GF Handel)
I know that my redeemer liveth,
And that he shall stand at the latter day upon the earth,
And though worms destroy this body,

Yet in my flesh shall I see God.
For now is Christ risen from the dead,
The first fruits of them that sleep.

REFLECTION *A Candlemas Creed* (adapted)
I have come to believe,
that on the Day of Resurrection,
when the Lord comes to wake us from sleep,
we may be surprised to discover that those who knew
a greater portion of darkness and despair in this world
have been up since cockcrow.
Those who had so little of this life's joy
and most of its sorrow will have
that little bit more of eternal life,
love and light than the rest of us.
On that great day the prodigality of the Father
will shock us out of our slumber again.
But we will be angry no more —
when we will see face to face
those whom we loved and lost a while.

II – Comfort

SONG Abide with Me (Lyte / Monk)

REFLECTION
All who saw her knew a queen
Upon a throne of youthful bliss:
A gifted nymph of seventeen
Safe from Hades' serpent hiss.
Her parents doted on their miss
Who filled the air with beauty's gift:

Her face was like the sunshine's kiss;
Her wit and laugh were passing swift.
None could guess the mental drift
That told her life was all in vain.
No friend could span the widening rift
'Twixt outer smile and inner pain.
Till she cured her world of all its ills
With a bottle full of sleeping pills.

SONG Healer of My Soul (John Michael Talbot)

READING John 11:17-27

On arriving in Bethany, Jesus found that Lazarus had been in the tomb for four days already. Bethany is only about two miles from Jerusalem, and many Jews had come to Martha and Mary to comfort them about their brother. When Martha heard that Jesus was coming, she went to meet him. Mary remained sitting in the house. Martha said to Jesus, 'Lord, if you had been here, my brother would not have died, but even now I know that God will grant whatever you ask of him'. Jesus said to her, 'Your brother will rise again'. Martha said, 'I know that he will rise again at the resurrection on the last day'. Jesus said to her, 'I am the resurrection. Anyone who believes in me, even though that person dies, will live, and whoever lives and believes in me will never die. Do you believe this?' 'Yes, Lord', she said, I believe that you are the Christ, the Son of God, the one who was to come into this world.'

TESTIMONY 1
This is given by someone, bereaved by suicide, who has walked this road of sadness.

SONG The God of Life (Liam Lawton)

God we believe in your tender love for us.

Give comfort and strength to those who mourn today.

Take away any feeling of guilt and ease the burden of regret.

Keep them in your care and help them to renew their lives in a spirit of trust.

We ask this in faith, through Christ, Our Lord. Amen.

III – Circle of Hope

READING Mark 15:33-37

When the sixth hour came there was darkness over the whole land until the ninth hour. And at the ninth hour Jesus cried out in a loud voice, 'Eloi, Eloi, lama sabachtani?, which means, 'My God, my God, why have you forsaken me?' When some of those who stood by heard this, they said, 'Listen, he is calling on Elijah'. Someone ran and soaked a sponge in vinegar and, putting it on a reed, gave it him to drink saying, 'Wait! And see if Elijah will come to take him down'. But Jesus gave a loud cry and breathed his last.

TESTIMONY 2

Words of understanding and empathy from someone who has been to the brink of suicide.

SONG My God, My God (Marty Haugen)

TESTIMONY 3

Words of hope and enlightenment. This may be the same speaker as for Testimony 2.

HOPE

Instrumental music is played, as some candles from the Cross are formed into a circle of hope. The music continues, while the intercessions are read.

INTERCESSIONS

We remember those who have taken their own lives:
May they come to know the tender compassion of the God who created them in love.

We lift up to the Lord those bereaved by the suicide of someone they love:
As they continue their journey may they meet Christ in the support of others.

We pray in hope for all gathered here:
May the Spirit of God open our ears to each other and may the circle of light generated through this service shine in the dark places of our lives.

CONCLUDING PRAYER *Daily Candlemas Prayer* (Adapted)

Lord,
You are the Saviour of those who trust in you.
You are the God of the humble,
the help of the oppressed,
the support of the weak,
the refuge of the forsaken,
the Saviour of the despairing.
Please hear our prayer this day.
Good Shepherd, lift our burden of isolation,
loneliness and depression.

In our turmoil, pain and anguish let us know
that we are loved and accepted by you.
As the Good Shepherd you are searching for us
to carry us in your arms.

Jesus, our burden can never be too heavy for you;
you carried the cross of shame and humiliation.
surround us with your protecting love
and lead us to confide our pain to another – Someone.

SONG Be Not Afraid   (Bob Dufford)

Remember Those Who Cannot Remember

Prayer and Ritual for Those Affected by Alzheimer's Disease

Introduction

Alzheimer's Disease is a reality for many families, as it affects more than 50,000 men and women in Ireland today. Those suffering from Alzheimer's Disease initially experience increasing memory loss, confusion and wandering, then severe disorientation, speech loss and finally complete physical and emotional helplessness. The disease has no known cure and there is no effective treatment.

The trauma experienced by carers of people afflicted by this illness is even greater. They are forced to make enormous personal and financial sacrifices along the way and must watch their loved ones deteriorate before their eyes, knowing that their heart-breaking ordeal will only come to an end with the death of the one they love. Without support, the burden of care, and the loneliness and isolation experienced by the carer can seem intolerable. This service offers support to carers, prayer for all affected by this illness and an opportunity to promote awareness of the disease.

This liturgy uses four mimes to illustrate the progress of the condition and its effects on the carers and those who suffer with the illness: Independence, Isolation, Support and Peace. These four mimes lead to a reflection for each stage of the liturgy.

SONG Remember Your Love (The Dameans)

WELCOME
A representative of a local Alzheimer's support group or care centre welcomes those present and may give the practical context for the celebration.

OPENING PRAYER
Let us pray,
God of mercy and compassion be with us today
as we gather to remember those who cannot remember.
We lift up to you their confusion and their pain.
We pray for the carers that they may have the strength to continue their blessed work and that they may receive the respite and support they need.
May we as a community recognise our responsibility to provide for those affected by Alzheimer's Disease.
We ask this, in the Spirit, through Christ Our Lord. *Amen.*

MIME Independence

This first scene shows an active couple moving through their neighbourhood, being greeted by friends and generally presenting an ordinary experience of life.

READING John 21:18-19
In all truth I tell you,
when you were young
you put on your own belt
and walked where you liked;
but when you grow old
you will stretch out your hands,
and somebody else will put a belt round you
and take you where you would rather not go.

SONG On Eagle's Wings   (Michael Joncas)

MIME Isolation

This second scene shows one of the two obviously disoriented and confused, trying to find the way home. The other partner is distraught at the door of their home.

REFLECTION   *Beatitudes for the Aged*
Blessed are they who understand
My faltering steps and palsied hand.
Blessed are they who know that my ears today
Must strain to catch the things they say.
Blessed are they who seem to know
That my eyes are dim and my wits are slow.
Blessed are they with a cheery smile
Who stop to chat for a little while.
Blessed are they who never say

'You've told that story twice today'.
Blessed are they who know the ways
To bring back memories of yesterdays.
Blessed are they who make it known
That I am loved, respected, and not alone.
Blessed are they who know I am at a loss
To find the strength to carry the cross.
Blessed are they who ease the days
On my journey Home in loving ways.

SONG Come to Me (Michael Joncas)

PRAYER   The Lord's Prayer

MIME Support
The couple are seen walking down the road, one clearly supporting the other. Unsure of how to react, neighbours avoid them – and it hurts. A representative of the Alzheimer's Association leads them to a support centre and some practical relief.

REFLECTION *A Wife's Prayer for Her Husband*
He was once so strong and capable
So functional and so free,
Oh, what has happened may I ask
To the husband so dear to me?
Why are his thoughts so tangled?
Nothing is ever the same.
Why does he look so vague
And his shuffling steps so lame?
He cannot remember from day to day
And all his skills are lost
He's fully aware it is happening

And doesn't know the terrible cost.
He has not much concentration
And can no longer read and write,
And now he cannot tell the time
And has lost some hearing and sight!
But the change in his personality
Has been very hard to bear,
He is very much dependent
Needs lots of loving care.
For he suffers progressive dementia
Which is robbing him of his mind.
And I pray to God in Heaven
Someday sweet peace he'll find.

SONG The Clouds' Veil (Liam Lawton)

REFLECTION *To My Mother, Old and Forgetful*
It's time to leave and I hug you,
All that is you in my life –
As I let it go.

I leave the world as new,
when snowdrops were new, and puppies,
and travel and books!
And my own body was new, my clothes and shoes,
Because I was growing.

I leave my sense of home;
your tweeds, and brooches,
the paintings you did of trees,
Your old desk and three-cornered chair,
The green and white vase for flowers
from the garden you made wherever you lived.

Your voice that speaks my name –
Your hands, the way they loved my children,
and showed it in deeds, over and over.
Before my memory worked
I lived in you, in your mind.
Now I do the remembering,
And tell you who you were, where you are
And what we are doing now.
As I leave you – receding into the future,
It will coil and join up with the past,
And we'll be together, as always.

SONG The Bells of the Angelus (French)

MIME Peace
*The refrain of 'The Clouds' Veil' is taken up again, as a Christ figure
emerges from behind a muslin veil and embraces the couple. A spirit of deep
peace comes over both of them.*

PRAYER *All*
God grant me the serenity
To accept the things I cannot change,
Courage to change the things I can,
And the wisdom to know the difference.

SONG All Will Be Well (Steven C. Warner)

HOMILY
*The homily leads into a period of prayerful reflection, which may be
accompanied by some instrumental music.*

CONCLUDING PRAYER

O loving Father, who gave Your only Son, Jesus Christ, to suffer and die for our sake, we humbly ask you to comfort all those who are afflicted by Alzheimer's Disease or any other form of dementia. Help them to know Your all embracing love and to find Your peace.

Grant understanding and patience to their families and friends. Help them to maintain their loving care until the end. Comfort them then with the knowledge that their loved one suffers no longer and is gone from this world, to be nearer to You.

Bless the work of the Alzheimer Society of Ireland, its national council, regional committees, branches, support groups and all its members and friends.

We ask this in the name of Your Son, Our Saviour, Jesus Christ. *Amen.*

FINAL SONG Lord Of All Hopefulness   (Struther/Gaelic)

Remember Them

A Service of Remembrance for the Month of November

Across simply adorned with flowers is the central focus of this service. People are invited to write the names of those they wish to be remembered in a book as they come in the door. They also receive a night light, which will be lit during the ceremony from the Paschal Candle.

OPENING SONG The Day You Gave Us (Ellerton/Scholefield)

OPENING PRAYER

Almighty God,

Through the death of your Son on the cross

You destroyed our death;

Through his rest in the tomb

You hallowed the graves of all who believe in you;

And through his rising again you restored us to eternal life.

God of the living and the dead

Accept our prayers for those who have died in Christ

And are buried with him in the hope of rising again.

Since they were true to your name on earth,

Let them praise you for ever in the joy of heaven.

We ask this through Christ, our Lord. Amen.

RESPONSORIAL PSALM In You Lord (Paul Inwood)
        or Mo Ghrá Thú A Thiarna (Liam Lawton)

READING Philippians 2:5-11

Make your own the mind of Christ Jesus: Who, being in the form of God, did not count equality with God something to be grasped. But he emptied himself, taking the form of a slave, becoming as human beings are; and being in every way like a human being, he was humbler yet, even to accepting death, death on a cross. And for this God raised him high, and gave him the name which is above all other names; so that all beings in the heavens, on earth and in the underworld, should bend the knee at the name of Jesus and that every tongue should acknowledge Jesus Christ as Lord, to the glory of God the Father.

SONG Christus Factus Est (Palestrina) or Per Crucem (Taizé)

REFLECTION *Autumn Churchyard*

Do not search for me down among the marble headstones
Where rooks on November branches
Make gathering cry for the dying year.
Do not look for me where summers leaves
Decay on waves of winter grass.
Do not imagine me as you last saw me
Pale, bruised and empty of life.
I am not here
But see that shaft of sunlight
Which spots the grey dark lake of late November
On the heather hillside of Donegal
Or listen to the thrush
Squeeze out the last notes of its sunny summer song.
Or hear the laughter
I splashed in my sisters face
On the sun drenched beach that summer before I left you.
I go on playing not where winter withers
But where spring
Is eternal.

      (John McCullagh)

SONG Chorale from Cantata No. 161   (J. S. Bach)
     or Ag Críost an Síol   (Seán Ó Riada)

READING John 17:1-4

Jesus raised his eyes to heaven and said:
Father, the hour has come: glorify your Son so that your Son may glorify you; so that, just as you have given him power over all humanity, he may give eternal life to all those you have entrusted to him. And eternal life is this: to know you, the only true God, and Jesus Christ whom you have sent. I have glorified you on earth by finishing the work that you gave me to do.

REFLECTION *Compassion*

They arrived at the appointed place
where He who bore all crosses stood,
welcoming saint and sinner with open arms.
He lifted the burden from each one's shoulder
And placed it in a circle around the Cross,
Which He for us had borne.
They sat around in silence.
And as His gaze looked with love into each heart
they knew instinctively that He knew and understood
the weight and burden of the crosses they carried.
He spoke in tongues but no sound came,
yet each one heard His words within the heart,
which changed the weight and texture of the crosses they carried.
He then raised His hands and gave a blessing.
And then He gave a strange direction and a choice –
whoever wished could exchange their cross for His,
or for the cross of those who had caused them pain,
or they could embrace their own,
now transformed with compassionate love.
And if they were to travel further with Him
in the peace and joy they now experienced,
they must allow his compassion to flow,
which forgave the other
and sought forgiveness for themselves.
Strange as it may seem
none of them exchanged their crosses for His
and few if any took the crosses of their afflictors.
Those who did left them down again
for they realised that they were very heavy,

that their own crosses
fitted their own shoulders best
for the rest of the journey home.
　　　(Frank Fahey)

CEREMONY AROUND THE CROSS
The people come forward with night lights and place them around the cross.
Each person then receives a bookmark with an image of the cross on it. One
of the following is sung while this is taking place.

SONG Jesus Remember Me (Taizé) or Lead Me Lord (S.S. Wesley)

INTERCESSIONS
For all who mourn today:
That they may feel the healing power of Christ in the midst of
their pain and grief.
Let us pray to the Lord: Lord, hear our prayer.

For those whom we remember at this time:
In baptism they were given the pledge of eternal life, may they
now be admitted to the company of the saints.
Let us pray to the Lord: Lord, hear our prayer.

Guímid go dtabharfaidh Dia síocháin agus solas suthain do na
firéin uile.
A Thiarna, éist linn. A Thiarna, bí ceansa agus éist linn.

For the whole Church:
That we may prepare worthily for the hour of our death, when
God will call us by name to pass from this world to the next.
Let us pray to the Lord: Lord, hear our prayer.

CALLING OF NAMES

Depending on the number of names to be called out, one or more readers slowly call out the names that have been written in the book of remembrance.

SONG There Is A Place (Liam Lawton)

CONCLUDING PRAYER

Lord God,
Whose days are without end
And whose mercies beyond counting,
Keep us mindful that life is short and the hour of death unknown.
Let your Spirit guide our days on earth
In the ways of holiness and justice,
That we may serve you in union with the whole Church,
Sure in faith, strong in hope, perfect in love.
And when our earthly journey is ended,
Lead us rejoicing into your kingdom,
Where you live for ever and ever. *Amen.*

FINAL SONG Abide With Me (Monk/Lyte)

Who Cares for the Carers?

Reflections on Caring Today

'I would like to meet each of you, in every place on earth, to bless you in the name of Jesus Christ, who went about "doing good and healing" the sick (Acts 10:38). I would like to be at your side to console you in your afflictions, sustain your courage, nourish your hope, that all of you may be able to make yourselves a gift of love to Christ for the good of the Church and the world.'

> (Holy Father's Message for the Second World Day of the Sick, 1994)

TO BE A CHRISTIAN IS TO CARE

To care for the needy and dependent is to be truly Christian. In His lifetime Jesus singled out sick and disabled people for special attention and stressed that those who care for them, care for Him. '... Just as you did it to one of the least of these who are members of my family, you did it to me' (Mt 25:40).

The Christian message is clear – Reach out and care for those who are less fortunate when we have health, resources and means to do so. In a sense, the need for care is universal – we all have needed and received care at some time in our lives. We still need and receive care in many, often unrecognised, ways. But some are more needy than others, for example, the sick, people suffering from physical and mental disability and the frail elderly.

CARE AND CARING IN IRELAND

In Ireland today, families are the prime care-givers. We know for example that only five percent of older people are institutionalised. The vast majority live at home. On the whole, they are well and independent. A number, however, need care and companionship. In addition, many chronically ill and disabled people are cared for full-time at home. It is estimated that there are approximately 100,000 informal carers in Ireland at present, 66,000 of whom care for older dependent relatives.

ARE YOU A CARER?

Are you looking after a family member or neighbour?

Is your life restricted because someone – an elderly parent, a sick child, a sibling, a disabled spouse – is at home, waiting for you to come in, depending on you for a meal, for bed care, for company?

Do you sometimes wonder how and why this situation came about?

Do you sometimes wonder if anybody else realises the extent of the stress of caring?

Do you sometimes feel you simply cannot go on?

Are you surprised, even shocked, when you feel frustrated, angry, guilty, isolated, abandoned even – because deep down, you do want to care?

Do you at times, feel like screaming – 'Does anybody out there care about me in my caring?'

THE BURDEN OF CARE AND SUPPORT FOR CARERS

There is a growing awareness that most family care is done by family members and neighbours. Government Departments –

especially the Department of Health and Children and the Department of Social, Community and Family Affairs – Health Board Personnel and the general public accept that, despite a developing care-service for older people, informal carers are carrying the bulk of the burden of care.

Family care is often taken for granted because families have always cared for their dependent and sick relatives out of a sense of love, care and duty. Most carers do not ask for help even though caring is becoming more difficult owing to increasing numbers of older and dependent people in the population. But, we all know people whose lives are made difficult by the task of caring.

COULD YOU HELP IN ANY WAY?

– By shopping?
– By sitting with a dependent or housebound person for a few hours, thus relieving the regular carer?
– By helping with meals and laundry?
– By being available to drive the carer to the shops, or to bring the dependent person to Mass or on a social outing?
– By setting up a parish Carers' Support Group?

WHAT SERVICES AND HELP ARE AVAILABLE FOR CARERS?

For advice, information and medical services, contact your local GP or Public Health Nurse. Respite Care (a break for the older person or the carer) can be arranged also through GPs and Public Health Nurses.

Circle Of Care

The Sick, Christ and the Carers

OPENING SONG Lord of All Hopefulness (Struther/Gaelic)

OPENING PRAYER

Tender and compassionate God,
Your Son, Jesus, always had a special welcome for the sick.
We are his hands, reaching out to those in need of healing and
peace in our communities. May we imitate his example in caring
for those who are broken or wounded.

In the wonder of the Trinity you live in never-ending love, with
your Son and the Holy Spirit. Let our outreach to the sick reflect
that love in a seamless circle of care. You who live and reign for
ever and ever. *Amen.*

I – The Sick

INTRODUCTION by Father Maurice Reidy
Within our community, there are few who are not touched in some way by the experiences of sickness or trauma. We only have to reflect for a moment to realise how immediate are those experiences, even within our own families. Ill-health is no respecter of persons, from the young to the elderly, tragedy strikes at random, impairing or taking away physical or mental ability. There are no concerns that are not the concerns of each of us when it comes to issues of health and well-being. Loss, whether through the death of a loved one or the realisation of human fragility, strikes to the core, throwing us into a lonely cycle of uncertainty and grief.

Those of us who grapple with the reality of suffering and impairment frequently feel isolated and separated from others. This is true, also, of those who are our carers. More than ever, there is a need for the experience of confirmation and community which supports us in coping with the stresses and distresses of disability and of bereavement, enabling us to meet the new challenges to live in faith, hope and love.

Those of us who minister to people who suffer in body or in mind, or to those who care for them, need to be open to their experiences and to their questions. We need to be open, also, to learn from their strengths and their wisdoms wrought in pain.

REFLECTIONS
A Child's Prayer
God bless all the nurses
Who try to make us well
They always come running
When we ring the bell.
God bless all the doctors
And the television in our room

God bless all the cleaning ladies
Who come round with their broom.
(Adrian, age 12)

Lord, If Only You Could Listen
Lord, if only you could listen and hear confusion in my mind,
Would you break down and cry for me,
Would you break down and die for me?
And Lord, if you could know the feeling when life begins to get
me down,
Would you break down and cry for me,
Would you break down and die for me?
And Lord, to live from day to day,
Would never help me find my way,
O Lord will you take my hand and lead me there,
To your side forever, ever my Lord?

Beatitudes for the Aged
Blessed are they who understand
My faltering steps and palsied hand.
Blessed are they who know that my ears today
Must strain to catch the things they say.
Blessed are they who seem to know
That my eyes are dim and my wits are slow.
Blessed are they with a cheery smile
Who stop to chat for a little while.
Blessed are they who never say
'You've told that story twice today'.
Blessed are they who know the ways
To bring back memories of yesterdays.
Blessed are they who make it known
That I am loved, respected, and not alone.
Blessed are they who know I am at a loss

To find the strength to carry the cross.
Blessed are they who ease the days
On my journey Home in loving ways.

PRAYER *All*
God grant me the serenity
To accept the things I cannot change,
Courage to change the things I can,
And the wisdom to know the difference.

II – Jesus Christ

SONG Christ Be Beside Me (James Quinn / Gaelic)

READING Mark 2:1-12
(This story can be told creatively using Transformations, *by the Brothers Pennington, on CD and cassette.)*

READING Mark 2:1-12
When Jesus returned to Capernaum, some time later word went round that he was in the house; and so many people collected that there was no room left, even in front of the door. He was preaching the word to them when some people came bringing him a paralytic carried by four men, but as they could not get the man to him through the crowd, they stripped the roof over the place where Jesus was; and when they had made an opening, they lowered the stretcher on which the paralytic lay. Seeing their faith, Jesus said to the paralytic, 'My child, your sins are forgiven.' Now some scribes were sitting there, and they thought to themselves, 'How can this man talk like that? He is being blasphemous. Who but God can forgive sins?' And at once, Jesus, inwardly aware that this is what they were thinking, said to them, 'Why do you have these thoughts in your hearts? Which of these is easier: to say to the paralytic, "Your sins are forgiven" or to say, "Get up, pick up your stretcher and walk"? But to

prove to you that the Son of man has authority to forgive sins on earth' – he said to the paralytic – 'I order you: get up, pick up your stretcher, and go off home.' And the man got up, and at once picked up his stretcher and walked out in front of everyone, so that they were all astonished and praised God saying, 'We have never seen anything like this.'

PRAYER
Jesus, our hope and our strength,
We thank you for your presence in our lives, especially at difficult moments. Help us to face each day with trust in your healing and comforting presence. *Amen.*

SONG The Deer's Cry (Shaun Davey)

III – The Carers

ADDRESS
The address could be given by someone who is a carer or who has experience of working with carers.

SONG Saint Teresa's Prayer (John Michael Talbot)

PRAYER The Lord's Prayer

Concluding Prayer
Father of tenderness and compassion,
you sent your Son to share our human nature,
to redeem all people, and to heal the sick.
Look with love on all and those who are sick.
Support them with your power,
give them hope in times of suffering
and keep them always in your care.
We ask this through Christ, our Lord. *Amen.*

CONCLUDING SONG Christ Be Our Light (Bernadette Farrell)

World Day of the Sick 1993

Message of the Holy Father for the First World Day of the Sick

DEAR BROTHERS AND SISTERS,

1. The Christian community has always paid particular attention to the sick and the world of suffering in its multiple manifestations. In the wake of such a long tradition, the universal Church, with a renewed spirit of service, is preparing to celebrate the first World Day of the Sick as a special occasion for growth, with an attitude of listening, reflection, and effective commitment in the face of the great mystery of pain and illness. This Day, which, beginning in February 1993, will be celebrated every year on the commemoration of Our Lady of Lourdes, for all believers seeks to be 'an intense moment of prayer, sharing, offering suffering for the good of the Church, and a call for everyone to recognise in the face of our sick brother the Holy Face of Christ, who, in suffering, dying, and rising again, carried out the salvation of humanity' *(Letter Instituting the World Day of the Sick,* May 13, 1992, no.3) The Day seeks, moreover, to involve all men of good will. Indeed, the basic questions posed by the reality of suffering and the appeal to bring both physical and spiritual relief to the sick do not concern believers alone, but interpellate all mankind, marked by the limits of the mortal condition.

2. Unfortunately, we are preparing to celebrate this first World Day in circumstances which are in some respects dramatic: the events of these months, while bringing out the urgency of prayer to entreat divine aid, recall us to the duty of implementing new and swift measures to assist those who suffer and cannot wait.

3. Before the eyes of all are the very sad images of individuals and whole peoples who, lacerated by wars and conflicts, succumb under the weight of easily avoidable calamities. How can we turn our gaze from the imploring faces of so many human beings, especially children, reduced to a shell of their former selves by the hardships of every kind in which they are caught up against their will because of egoism and violence? And how can we forget all those who at health-care facilities – hospitals, clinics, leprosariums, centres for the disabled, nursing homes – or in their own dwellings undergo the Calvary of sufferings which are often neglected, not always suitably relieved, and sometimes even aggravated by a lack of adequate support?

4. Illness, which in everyday experience is perceived as a frustration of the natural life force, for believers becomes an appeal to 'read' the new, difficult situation in the perspective which is proper to faith. Outside of faith, moreover, how can we discover in the moment of trial the constructive contribution of pain? How can we give meaning and value to the anguish, unease, and physical and psychic maladies accompanying our mortal condition? What justification can we find for the decline of old age and the final goal of death, which, in spite of all scientific and technological progress, inexorably remain?

Yes, only in Christ, the incarnate Word, redeemer of man and victor over death, is it possible to find the satisfactory answer to such fundamental questions. In the light of Christ's death and resurrection, illness no longer appears as an exclusively negative event – rather, it is seen as a 'visit by God', an opportunity 'to release love, to make works of love towards one's neighbour arise, to transform all human civilisation into the civilisation of love' (Apostolic Letter, *Salvifici Doloris*, 30).

The history of the Church and of Christian spirituality offers very broad testimony of this. Over the centuries shining pages have been written of heroism in suffering accepted and offered in union with Christ. And no less marvellous pages have been traced out through humble service to the poor and the sick, in whose tormented flesh the presence of the poor, crucified Christ has been recognised.

5. The World Day of the Sick – in its preparation, realisation, and objectives – is not meant to be reduced to a mere external display centring on certain initiatives, however praiseworthy they may be, but is intended to reach consciences to make them aware of the valuable contribution which human and Christian service to those suffering makes to better understanding among men and, consequently, to building real peace.

Indeed, peace presupposes, as its preliminary condition, that special attention be reserved for the suffering and the sick by public authorities, national and international organisations, and every person of good will. This is valid, first of all, for developing countries – in Latin America, Africa, and Asia – which are marked by serious deficiencies in health care. With the celebration of the World Day of the Sick, the Church is promoting a renewed commitment to those populations, seeking to cancel out the injustice existing today by devoting greater human, spiritual, and material resources to their needs.

In this regard, I wish to address a special appeal to civil authorities, to men of science, and to all those who work in direct contact with the sick. May their service never become bureaucratic and aloof! Particularly, may it be quite clear to all that the administration of public money imposes the serious duty of avoiding its waste and improper use so that available resources, administered wisely and equitably, will serve to ensure prevention of disease and care during illness for all who need them.

The hopes which are so alive today for a humanisation of medicine and health care require a more decisive response. To make healthcare more humane and adequate it is, however, essential to draw on a transcendent vision of man which stresses the value and sacredness of life in the sick person as the image and Son of God. Illness and pain affect every human being: love for the suffering is the sign and measure of the degree of civilisation and progress of a people.

6. To you, dear sick people all over the world, the main actors of this World Day, may this event bring the announcement of the living and comforting presence of the Lord. Your sufferings, accepted and borne with unshakeable faith, when joined to those of Christ, take on extraordinary value for the life of the Church and the good of humanity.

For you, health workers called to the highest, most meritorious and exemplary testimony of justice and love, may this Day be a renewed spur to continue in your delicate service with generous openness to the profound values of the person, to respect for human dignity, and to defence of life, from its beginning to its natural close.

For you, Pastors of the Christian people, and to all the different members of the Church community, for volunteers, and particularly for those engaged in the healthcare ministry, may this World Day of the Sick offer stimulus and encouragement to go forward with fresh dedication on the way of service to tired, suffering man.

7. On the commemoration of Our Lady of Lourdes, whose sanctuary at the foot of the Pyrenees has become a temple of human suffering, we approach – as she did on Calvary, where the cross of her Son rose up – the crosses of pain and solitude of so many brothers and sisters to bring them comfort, to share their suffering and present it to the Lord of life, in spiritual communion with the whole Church.

May the Blessed Virgin, 'Health of the Sick' and 'Mother of the Living', be our support and our hope and, through the celebration of the Day of the Sick, increase our sensitivity and dedication to those being tested, along with the trusting expectation of the luminous day of our salvation, when every tear will be dried forever (cf. Is 25:8). May it be granted to us to enjoy the first fruits of that day from now on in the superabundant joy – though in the midst of all tribulations (cf. 2 Cor. 7:4) – promised by Christ can take from us (Jn 16:22).

I extend my Blessing to all!

FROM THE VATICAN, OCTOBER 21 1992.

JOHN PAUL II.

World Day of the Sick 2000

Message Of The Holy Father for World Day Of The Sick, 2000

1. The Eighth *World Day of the Sick* will be held in Rome on 11 February 2000, the year of the *Great Jubilee*, and will find the Christian community dedicated to re-examining the reality of illness and suffering in the perspective of the mystery of the Incarnation of the Son of God, to draw from this extraordinary event new light to illumine these basic human experiences.

At the end of the second millennium of the Christian era, as the Church looks with admiration at humanity's progress in the treatment of suffering and improved health care, she is paying attention to the questions raised by the health-care sector, the better to define her presence in this context and to respond appropriately to the pressing challenges of the time.

Throughout history, people have made the most of their intellectual and emotional resources to overcome the limits inherent in the human condition, and have made great breakthroughs in health care. It is enough to think of the possibility of prolonging life and improving its quality, of alleviating suffering and of increasing a person's potential through the use of good, reliable medicines and increasingly sophisticated technologies. In addition to these achievements are those of a social kind, such as the widespread awareness of the right to treatment and its expression in juridical terms in the various 'Charters of the rights of the sick'. Nor should we forget the significant development achieved in the area of assistance due to the emergence of new medical applications, of a nursing service which is ever better qualified and of the phenomenon of voluntary service, which has recently reached a high degree of competence.

2. However, at the end of the second millennium we cannot say that humanity has done all that is necessary to alleviate the immense burden of suffering which weighs on individuals, families and entire societies.

On the contrary, it seems that, especially in this last century, the river of human pain, already swollen due to the frailty of human nature and the wound of original sin, as well as the suffering inflicted by the mistakes of individuals and of States, has broadened: I am thinking of the wars that have caused so much bloodshed in this century, perhaps more than in any other in humanity's tormented history: I am thinking of the types of disease that are prevalent in society such as drug dependency, AIDS, illnesses caused by the deterioration of the big cities and the environment; I am thinking of the increase in organised crime, both small- and large-scale, and of the proposals of euthanasia.

I have a mental picture not only of the hospital beds in which so many of the sick are lying, but also of the sufferings of refugees, orphaned children and the many victims of social evils and poverty. At the same time, with the eclipse of faith, especially in the secularised world, there is a further serious cause of suffering, that of no longer being able to grasp the salvific meaning of pain and the comfort of eschatological hope.

3. Sharing in the joys and hopes, sorrows and anxieties of the people of every age, the Church has constantly accompanied and sustained humanity in its struggle against pain and its commitment to improve health. At the same time, she has striven to reveal to mankind the meaning of suffering and the riches of the Redemption brought by Christ the Saviour. History records great men and women who, prompted by their desire to imitate Christ through a

deep love for their poor and suffering brethren, started countless initiatives of social assistance, brightening the last two millenniums with good works.

Next to the Fathers of the Church and the founders and foundresses of religious institutes, how can we fail to wonder at and admire the countless people who, in silence and humility, have given their lives in service to their sick neighbour, in many cases to point of heroism. (cf. *Vita consecrata*, n. 83). Daily experience shows how the Church, inspired by the Gospel of charity, continues to contribute with many works, hospitals, health-care structures and volunteer organisations, to promoting health and to caring for the sick, paying special attention to the most underprivileged in all parts of the world, notwithstanding the cause of their suffering, whether voluntary or involuntary.

This presence should be maintained and encouraged for the benefit of the precious good of human health, looking carefully at all the inequalities and contradictions in the world of health-care that still exists.

4. Indeed, down the centuries, beside the light areas, shadows have obscured and still obscure the overall picture of improvements in health care, many aspects of which are truly fine. I am thinking in particular of the serious social inequalities in access to health-care resources, which are still present in vast areas of the world, especially in the countries of the South.

This unjust inequality is more and more dramatically undermining the basic rights of the person: entire populations do not even have the possibility of benefiting from primary, basic medicines, while elsewhere even expensive medicines are widely wasted and misused. And what can be said of the many brothers and sisters who lack the minimum to appease their hunger and are subject to every kind of disease. Not to mention the numerous wars which stain humanity with blood and are spreading physical psychological traumas of every kind, as we well as death.

5. With regard to these scenarios, we must recognise that unfortunately, in many cases, the economic, scientific and technological breakthroughs have not brought real progress that is focused on the person and the inviolable dignity of every human being. Even the achievements in the field of genetics, which are fundamental in health care, especially for the protection of new-born life, can become an opportunity for inadmissible choices, callous manipulation and interests that contradict real development, often with devastating results.

On the one hand remarkable efforts are being made to prolong life and even to procreate it artificially; but on the other, birth is not permitted to those who have already been conceived, and the death of those no longer considered to be of use is hastened. Furthermore: while health is rightly appreciated with increasing initiatives to promote it, at times reaching a sort of cult of the body and a hedonistic quest for physical fitness, at the same time we are reduced to considering life as a mere consumer good, setting a new scale of marginalisation for the disabled, the elderly and the terminally ill.

All these contradictions and paradoxical situations stem from a lack of harmony on the one hand, between the logic and well-being and the search for technological progress, and the logic, on the other, of ethical values based on the dignity of every human being.

6. On the eve of the new millennium, it is hoped that 'the

purification of memory' will also be promoted in the world of suffering and the health, which will lead to 'recognising the wrongs done by those who have borne to bear the name of Christian' (*Incarnationis mysterium*, n. 11; cf. also *Tertio millennio adveniente*, nn. 33, 37, 51). The ecclesial community is called to accept, in this field too, the invitation to conversion which is linked to the celebration of the Holy Year.

The process of conversion and renewal will be helped if we continually raise our eyes to the One who, 'in the sacrament of the Eucharist took flesh in Mary's womb 20 centuries ago, (and) continues to offer himself to humanity as the source of divine life' (*Tertio millennio adveniente*, n. 55)

The mystery of the Incarnation means understanding life as a gift from God, to be looked after responsibly and used for good: health is thus a positive attribute of life, to be sought for the good of the person and of one's neighbour. However health is a 'penultimate' good in the hierarchy of values, which should be fostered and considered with a view to the total, and thus also spiritual, good of the person.

7. In this circumstance we turn our gaze in particular to the suffering and risen Christ. In taking on the human condition, the Son of God accepted to live it in all its aspects, including pain and death, fulfilling in his person the words he spoke at the Last Supper: 'Greater love has no man than this, that a man lay down his life for his friends' (Jn 15:13). In celebrating the Eucharist, Christians proclaim and share in the sacrifice of Christ, for 'by his wounds (we) have been healed' (cf. 1 Pt 2:24) and uniting themselves with him, 'preserve in their own suffering a very special particle of the infinite treasure of the worlds redemption, and can share this treasure with others' (*Salvifici doloris*, n. 27) The imitation of Jesus, the suffering

Servant, has led great saints and simple believers to turn their illnesses and pain into a source of purification and salvation for themselves and for others. What great prospects of personal sanctification and co-operation for the salvation of the world does the path marked out by Christ and by so many of his disciples open to our sick brothers and sisters! It is a difficult path, because the human being does not discover the meaning of suffering and death on his own, but it is always a possible path with the help of Jesus, interior Master and Guide (cf. *Salvifici doloris*, nn. 26-27).

Just as the Resurrection transformed Christ's wounds into a source of healing and salvation, so for every sick person the light of the risen Christ is a confirmation that the way of fidelity to God can triumph in the gift of self until the Cross and can transform illness itself into a source of joy and resurrection. Is not this the proclamation that echoes in hearts at every Eucharistic celebration when the people proclaim: 'Christ has died, Christ is risen, Christ will come again'? The sick, also sent out as labourers into the Lord's vineyard (cf. *Christifidelis laici*, n. 53), by their example can make an effective contribution to the evangelisation of a culture that tries to remove the experience of suffering by striving to grasp its deep meaning with its intrinsic incentives to human and Christian growth.

8. The Jubilee also invites us to contemplate the face of Jesus, *the divine Samaritan of souls and bodies*. By following the example of her divine Founder, the Church, 'from century to century has re-enacted the Gospel parable of the Good Samaritan, revealing and communicating her healing love and the consolation of Jesus Christ. This came about through the untiring commitment of the Christian community and all those who have taken care of the sick and suffering as well as the skilled and generous service of health-care workers' (*Christifideles laici*, n. 53). This commitment does not derive

from specific social situations nor should it be understood as an optional or fortuitous act, but is an intransgressible response to Christ's command: 'he called to him his twelve disciples and gave them authority over unclean spirits, to cast them out, and to heal every disease and every infirmity' (Mt 10: 1 cf. 7-8)

The service rendered to the person who is suffering in body and soul takes its meaning from the Eucharist, finding in it not only its source but also its norm. It was not by chance that Jesus closely united the Eucharist with service (Jn 13: 2-16), asking the disciples to perpetuate in memory of him not only the *'breaking of the bread'*, but also the *'washing of the feet'*.

9. The example of Christ, the good Samaritan, must inspire the believer's attitude, promoting him to be 'close' to his brothers and sisters who are suffering, through respect, understanding, acceptance, tenderness, compassion and gratuitousness. It is a question of fighting the indifference that makes individuals and groups withdraw selfishly into themselves. To this end, 'the family, the school and other educational institutions must, if only for humanitarian reasons, work perseveringly for the reawakening and refining of that sensitivity towards one's neighbour and his suffering' (*Salvifici doloris*, n. 29). For the believer, this human sensitivity is expressed in the agape, that is, in supernatural love, which brings one to love one's neighbour for love of God. In fact, guided by faith and surrounding with affectionate care those who are afflicted by human suffering, the Church recognises in them the image of her poor and suffering Founder and is concerned to alleviate their suffering, mindful of his words: 'I was sick and you visited me' (Mt 25:36). The example of Jesus, the good Samaritan, not only spurs one to help the sick, but also to do all one can to reintegrate him in society. For Christ, in fact, healing is also this reintegration: just as sickness excludes the human being from the

community, so healing must bring him to rediscover his place in the family, in the Church and in society.

I extend a warm invitation to those involved professionally or voluntarily in the world of health to fix their gaze on the divine Samaritan, so that their service can become a prefiguration of definitive salvation and a proclamation of new heavens and a new earth 'in which righteousness dwells' (2 Pt 3 :13).

10. Jesus did not only treat and heal the sick, but he was also a tireless *promoter of health* through his saving presence, teaching and action. His love for man was expressed in relationships full of humanity, which led him to understand, to show compassion and bring comfort, harmoniously combining tenderness and strength. He was moved by the beauty of nature, he was sensitive to human suffering, he fought evil and injustice. He faced the negative aspects of this experience courageously and, fully aware of the implications, communicated the certainty of a new world. In him the human condition showed its face redeemed and the deepest human aspirations found fulfilment

He wants to communicate this harmonious fullness of life to people today. His saving action not only aims to meet the needs of human people, victims of their own limits and errors, but to sustain their efforts for total self-fulfilment. He opens the prospect of divine life to man: 'I came that they may have life, and have it abundantly' (Jn 10:10).

Called to continue Jesus's mission, the Church must seek to promote a full and ordered life for everyone.

11. In the context of the promotion of good health and quality of life correctly understood, two duties deserve the Christian's special attention. First of all the *defence of life*. In today's world, many men

and women are striving for a better quality of life with respect for life itself and are reflecting on the ethics of life so as to dispel the confusion of values that sometimes exists in today's culture. As I recalled in my Encyclical *Evangelium vitae*, 'significant is the reawakening of an ethical reflection on issues affecting life. The emergence and ever more widespread development of bioethics is promoting more reflection and dialogue between believers and non-believers, as well as between followers of different religious ethical problems, including fundamental issues pertaining to human life' (n.27). However, beside these there are many, unfortunately who are engaged in promoting a worrying culture of death, spreading a mentality imbued with selfishness and hedonistic materialism, and with the social and legal sanction of the suppression of live.

At the root of this culture there is often a *Promethean attitude* which leads people to think that 'they can control life and death by taking the decisions about them into their own hands. What really happens in this case is that the individual is overcome and crushed by a death deprived of any prospect of meaning or hope' (*Evangelium vitae*, n. 15). When science and medical practice risk losing sight of their inherent ethical dimension, health-care professionals 'can be strongly tempted at times to become manipulators of life, or even agents of death' (ibid. n. 89).

12. In this context, believers are called to develop the insight of faith as they look at the sublime and mysterious value of life, even when it seems frail and vulnerable. 'This outlook does not give in to discouragement when confronted by those who are sick, suffering, outcast or at death's door. Instead, in all these situations it feels challenged to find meaning, and precisely in these circumstances it is open to perceiving in the face of every person a call to encounter, dialogue and solidarity' (ibid., n 83).

This task especially involves health professionals: doctors, pharmacists, nurses, chaplains, men and women religious, administrators and volunteer workers who, by virtue of their profession, are called in a special capacity to be guardians of human life. However, it also calls into question every other human being, starting with the relatives of the sick person. They know that 'the request which arises from the human heart in the supreme confrontation with suffering and death, especially when faced with the temptation to give up in utter desperation, is above all a request for companionship, sympathy and support in the time of trial. It is a plea for help to keep on hoping when all human hopes fail' (ibid., n 67).

13. The second duty which Christians cannot shirk *concerns the promotion of a health worthy of the human being*. In our society there is a risk of making health an idol to which every other value is subservient. The Christian vision of the human being opposes a notion of health reduced to pure, exuberant vitality and satisfaction with one's own physical fitness, far removed from any real consideration of suffering. This view, ignoring the person's spiritual and social dimensions, ends by jeopardising his true good. Precisely for growth and self-fulfilment, and opens the way to discovering new values.

The vision of health, based on an anthropology that respects the whole person, far from being identified with the mere absence of illness, strives to achieve a fuller harmony and health balance on the physical, psychological, spiritual and social level. In this perspective, the person himself is called to mobilise all his available energies to fulfil his own vocation and for the good of others.

14. This model of health requires that the Church and society create an *ecology worthy of man*. The environment, in fact, is connected with the health of the individual and of the population: it constitutes the human being's 'home' and the complex of resources entrusted to his care and stewardship, 'the garden to be tended and the field to be cultivated'. But the external ecology of the person must be combined with an interior, moral ecology, the only one which is fitting for a proper concept of health.

Considered in its entirety, human health thus becomes an attribute of life, a resource for the service one's neighbour and openness to salvation.

15. In the Jubilee year of the Lord's favour 'a year of the remission of sins and of the punishment due to them, a year of reconciliation between disputing parties, a year of manifold conversions and of sacramental and extra-sacramental penance' (*Tertio millennio adveniente*, n. 14) – I invite pastors, priests, men and women religious, the faithful and people of goodwill courageously to face the challenges that threaten the world of suffering and health.

May the *International Eucharistic Congress*, which will be celebrated in Rome in 2000, become the ideal centre, radiating prayers and initiatives that can make the divine Samaritan's presence alive and active in the world of health care. I fervently hope that through the contribution of our brothers and sisters in all the Christian Churches, the celebration of the Jubilee of the Year 2000 will mark the development of ecumenical collaboration in loving service to the sick, so as to witness clearly to everyone to the search for unity on the concrete path of charity.

I address a specific appeal to the international political, social and health-care organisations in every part of the world to be convincing promoters of concrete projects to fight all that is harmful to the dignity and health of the person.

May we be accompanied in the process of active participation in the lives of our sick brothers and sisters by the Virgin Mother who at the foot of the Cross (cf. Jn. 19:25) shared the sufferings of her Son, and with her expert experience of suffering, offers her constant and loving protection to those who are suffering in mind and body the limits and wounds of the human condition.

I entrust the sick and all those who are close to them to her, *Health of the sick and Queen of peace*, so that with her motherly intercession she will help them to build the civilisation of love.

With these hopes, I impart a special Apostolic Blessing to everyone.

From Castel Gandolfo, 6 August 1999, the Transfiguration of the Lord.

John Paul II

Music Sources

Seinn Alleluia 2000 (Columba, 1999)
Ag Críost an Síol (Seán Ó Riada)
Be Not Afraid (Bob Dufford)
Christ Be Beside Me (James Quinn)
Christ Be Our Light (Bernadette Farell)
Holy Mary, Full of Grace (Jean-Paul Lé cot)
Jesus Remember Me (Taizé)
Lord Of All Hopefulness (Slane)
Make Me A Channel Of Your Peace (Sebastian Temple)
Mo Ghrá Thó A Thiarna (Liam Lawton)
On Eagle's Wings (Michael Joncas)
Your Mercy Like Rain (Rory Cooney)
There Is A Place (Liam Lawton)

In Caelo (Veritas, 1999)
Healer of my Soul (John Michael Talbot)
See above
The God of Love (Liam Lawton)
The Clouds' Veil (Liam Lawton)
The Deer's Cry (Shaun Davey)
Lord of All Hopefulness (Stuther / Gaelic)
O Comfort My People (Crysogonous Waddell)
An tAiséirí (Traditional)

Gather Choir Book (GIA Publications, 1988)
Gather Us In (Marty Hangen)
My God, My God (Marty Hangen)
Remember Your Love (Damean Music)

Music From Taizé (HarperCollins *Religious, 1978*)
Jesus Remember Me
O Lord Hear My Prayer
The Lord is My Light
Christus Factus Est
Per Crucem